BRUSHES WITH

BRUSHES WITH

KRISTINA MARIE DARLING

BLAZEVOX[BOOKS]
Buffalo, New York

BRUSHES WITH
by Kristina Marie Darling
Copyright © 2013

Published by BlazeVOX [books]

Printed in the United States of America

Interior design and typesetting by Geoffrey Gatza
Cover Art: Visitation, by Noah Saterstrom, ink on paper, 9" x 9", 2012

First Edition
ISBN: 978-1-60964-146-7
Library of Congress Control Number: 2013942422

BlazeVOX [books]
131 Euclid Ave
Kenmore, NY 14217

Editor@blazevox.org

publisher of weird little books

BlazeVOX [books]

blazevox.org

21 20 19 18 17 16 15 14 13 12 01 02 03 04 05 06 07 08 09 10

BlazeVOX

ACKNOWLEDGEMENTS

The author would like to express her gratitude to the University at Buffalo. Thank you to Kyle McCord, Anne Champion, Geoffrey Gatza, Carol Guess, and Joe Hall for their friendship and encouragement. This book is for my family.

TABLE OF CONTENTS

BRUSHES WITH

~

"I watch the white stars darken;
the day comes and the
white stars dim
and lessen
and the lights fade in the city."
—H.D.

"There's a black rose growing in your garden."
—Anon.

~

CARTOGRAPHY

We were no longer in love. The sky, too, was beginning to show its wear. A silk lining could be seen through every slit in the dark green fabric.[1]

I started to wonder where we went wrong. You were holding a map of the constellations.[2] Each of the minor stars had been assigned to a square on a little grid. The map seemed scientific so I approached you.[3]

You kept looking down at your compass. The needle spinning beneath a little screw. Maybe this is where we went wrong.

Above us, the sky is still wearing its green dress. The most delicate strings holding it all in place.

---

[1] The photographs portray this dress as one of the most violent manifestations of the heroine's femininity.

[2] At the edge of the map, she could discern a cluster of minor stars. Their incessant movement seemed difficult to comprehend, let alone to document.

[3] "I had wanted to understand the cause of this fearful disturbance. Within my compass the needle kept spinning and spinning."

4. *Direction.*

      1. The management, supervision, or guidance of an operation.

      †2. The art of staging theatre.

      ‡3. A set of instructions for finding someone or something.

5. The science of cartography emerged as a discipline in ninth century Babylon, where pictures were drawn to illustrate the bitterness of the river where her beloved would later drown.

6. She kept the diagram in a locked box beneath the floorboards. The little silver hinges glittering beneath a ruined staircase.

7. The water-damaged portion of their correspondence, in which she describes her plan to debilitate and poison the hound that kept watch over his lavish country estate.

8. *Livraison.* Translated from the French as "delivery."

[9.] In the novel, she cannot bear the thought of him leaving, which explains the strange white residue visitors would later find on the windowsill.

MIGRATION

Before the broken compass, before that night in the desert, before the green dress unraveled, I was thinking of leaving.[10]

For years we had lived in a small chalet near the mountains; you could see the constellations more clearly there. We'd follow maps of the night sky and find ourselves in someone else's ruins, roaming a burial ground for dead stars.

The maps were always where we began. Their little grids and axes led us to conversations, and we'd contemplate the nature of things.

You told me that there was dark matter I couldn't see. That every star is a dead star.

I started to wonder if the maps had led us somewhere else. I bought a new compass, watched its needle, and tried to spin in place.

[10.] The little-known French film was often cited as evidence of the director's enduring interest in role reversals.

11. Upon breaking down the door, he discovered only an empty room. The rim of her teacup still gleaming on a silver service.

12. "He had threatened to unlock the mahogany cabinet. I didn't expect to see the sheet music, much less the maps and diagrams I had hidden from him."

13. Derived from the Swedish *gasa* ("to gape").

14. She wanted to understand the innermost workings of this elaborate machine. Their courtship appeared to her as a series of pulleys, levers, and strings. Behind a little door the machinery kept turning.

15. *Électric.* Translated from the French as "electric."

16. A late-nineteenth century stage play, in which the heroine falls in love with a generator.

17. See also Henry Adams' essay, "The Dynamo and the Virgin."

FEMINISM

After the divorce, after your mistress, after the stars were eclipsed by the bright lights of the city, I gathered all of the broken dishes you'd left behind. I placed each one of them on a little shelf, recorded their height in a dark green book.

I began to realize the significance of this gesture. What is love but a parade of memorable objects, a row of dead butterflies pinned under glass?

You had always loved mementos. Once you'd even rented a small boat to find your missing porcelain statuette.[18]

I started to wonder what other gifts you'd leave behind. The dried insects I'd find in each of your letters.

I closed the cabinet door, counted each piece of shattered glass, and tried to imagine them all in your perfect white hands.

[18.] This statue of the Holy Mother would later be found headless in a tiny museum in northern France.

[19] *Violence.*

  †1. The use of physical coercion.

  ‡2. The relative strength or duration of an emotion.

[20] She began referring to the affair as a "benevolent guillotine." The silver blades poised to kill.

[21] Beginning with Pre-Enlightenment philosophy, one is taught to view the world as a piece of well-designed machinery.

[22.] *Frigide.* Roughly translated as "frigid."

ANTARCTICA

When I mentioned the landscape, you were thinking of
something else.[23] All around us were figure skaters. The
blades on their shoes etching circles into the ice below.

For weeks we had been drifting apart. In each room of
the house, I imagined frost accumulating on the furniture.
An uncanny brightness in every window.

Now we're standing at the edge of the lake. You keep
telling me that you "need some more time." Your face
darkening like a house buried in winter.

So I sit down and try to carve a man from a block of ice.
In every direction, the same snow-covered fields.[24]

[23.] Variant opening:
> In even the smallest gesture, a declaration.

[24.] Throughout nineteenth century lyric poetry, the heroine's desires are
projected onto the meadow itself.

LANDSCAPE

You kept mentioning the other women, the way they
would lie on their backs in the grassy field. All around
them were breadknives. The place settings for a picnic.

But even before that we had been quarrelling. You told
me, tilting your pretty head, how my pastoral elegy failed
to move you.

Now you're watching women stare at the sky. Someone's
perfect clavicle showing through a white dress. The field
doesn't seem to end.

So I try and try to enter the landscape. I watch your
perfect mouth, mouthing commands: *threshold,*[25] *delicious,*[26]
melancholia.[27]

[25.] The boundary he had drawn between his carefully manicured garden and
her unruly terrain.

[26.] Meaning the physical sensation she experienced in the burned meadow.

[27.] A state of mourning for the lost object.

28. The documentary, filmed in the mysterious "house by the sea," follows its heroine through a series of dreams. Upon entering the corridor, she could only stare. The dark green dress had been scorched again and again in series of house fires.

29. "I had wanted to preserve the hemline, its flawless stitching. Now the lace cuff smolders and my violet nightdress burning in a locked room."

30. Critics have interpreted this recurring motif as an emblem for the heroine's attachment to the gatekeeper, who lived in a remote, and also inaccessible, "house by the sea."

31. Their brief correspondence has been likened to a tiny castle fraught with internal dissention.

32. "Upon reaching the top of the staircase, I could hardly speak. I stood near the window and watched the fire I had built around us."

33. *Souvenir.* Translated from the French as "recollection."

34. Throughout *Hamlet,* for example, the reader is reminded of the difference between "being" and "seeming."

35. This painting is the first in an ongoing series of depictions of the lovesick Ophelia. Here she appears as the victim of arson, her eyes widening as the fire grows uncontrollably around her.

36. "It was then I understood our exchange as a series of natural disasters. The smoke rising above the staircase was the first of these inexplicable acts of God. "

37. A lesser known order of nuns, who maintained an elaborate shrine to Saint Jude.

MARTYRDOM

I never imagined love as a cause for suicide. But there we were, surrounded by all of the tell-tale signs: a breadknife, a withered corsage, a white dress with some ruffles along the bottom.

The night before I sensed that something had gone terribly wrong. He told her, brushing the hair from his eyes, how her sonnets failed to *turn* at the volta.

Now she's gliding along the surface of the lake. Her hands folded like the knot on a small bouquet.

So he tries and tries to wake her. He looks at her perfect wrists, nearly submerged: cold skin,[38] a silver watch, every bracelet fastened in place.

[38.] The dark blue, and nearly frozen, flesh along her wrist has been interpreted as an emblem for her fiancé's almost scientific descriptions of the physical body.

39. "Until then I had maintained that one should strive for the height of precision. But the landscape seemed unmanageable, unruly even. Behind every door, the furniture burning in a locked room."

40. She would later discover his meticulous records of everything they had lost in the fire.

Still he tried to maintain some semblance of order. For every room in the house he had drafted an elaborate set of rules.

[42.] *Empire.*

1. Of, relating to, or characteristic of a neoclassic style, as in clothing or the decorative arts, prevalent in France during the first part of the 19th century.

†2. A political unit having an extensive territory or comprising a number of territories or nations and ruled by a single supreme authority.

‡3. Imperial or imperialistic sovereignty, domination, or control.

†4. A variety of apple having medium fruit with waxy, dark red skin and white flesh.

UTOPIA

Night.[45] The same bright red moon. And there we were, alone in the enormous house. You mentioned the iron latch on my door, how it made you think of a room somewhere in New England, but the windows weren't quite like that at all.

I smile and straighten the hem on my plain white dress. Cough and clear my throat to speak. That's when you look down at my patent leather shoes and tell me that Southerners are *always* so polite.

I begin rearranging furniture in the vestibule. Counting the little figurines I've amassed in glass cabinets.

The girls in these statues are always martyrs: drowned Ophelia, the Holy Mother, Jeanne D'Arc. Day after day the same shattered porcelain hands.

[45.] An emblem for the heroine's lack of practical, and thus useful, knowledge.

---

46. A scene in the documentary, in which the woman replies, "What he really loved was my ignorance."   Although an awkward silence ensued, the camera kept rolling for a few more minutes.

More than anything you loved a crowd. The rows of well-dressed women applauding your smallest gesture: the twitch beneath your eye, a cracked tooth, and on most days nothing at all.

So I smile and take my leave of the rapt faces below. Straighten the brim on my unsightly red hat. That's when I began to wonder what happened to the hound.

He would follow the guards and make sure they remained at the gate. Even in the midst of an insurrection. A clerk would later count the fingers on each of their carefully manicured hands.

I started to suspect the women had killed him. Because they're more vicious than we like to think: breadknives, shattered glass, and a loaded gun in some hidden back pocket.

Because day after day, you demand the same perfectly timed applause.[47]

[47.] This praise has been interpreted as an elaborate facade, beneath which nearly everyone sensed the beginnings of a revolution.

48. *Arsenal.*

    †1. A stock of weapons.

    ‡2. A store or supply.

49. A popular novel published at the height of the French Revolution, in which the heroine equates the sound of gunshots with her aging beloved's stuttering heartbeat.

50. "It was only then I understood the violence inherent in our brief exchange. It felt as though he had burned the note and sent the ashes in a cream-coloured envelope."

51. *Courier.* Translated from the French as "delivery."

52. Upon opening the parcel, she could barely speak. Her image suspended in a heap of shattered glass.

53. The film depicts a woman's attempts to interrogate the various men who had torn, defaced, or otherwise marked her handwritten letters.

54. A little known Greek myth, in which the gods of love and combat are etched onto opposing sides of the same white marble statue.

55. *Déclaration formelle de guerre.* In French politics, a formal declaration of war.

40

[56] By the end of that night, their enormous house had fallen into disrepair. In every window shattered glass where the light once was.

[57] This map of the constellations was used to navigate away from the physical site of combat, thus forming a circular arc as the boat approached the Arctic circle.

58. She remembered shivering in this mysterious "house by the sea." The wind circling all around her.

59. The dress, in its present state, could no longer be worn, let alone paraded as the heroine ascends a marble staircase.

60. In astronomy, this term refers to dark matter that can only be seen with a state-of-the-art sighting instrument.

62. This piece of machinery revealed as much as it seemed to conceal.

43

Upon seeing the smoke rising, she could barely speak. The little statue lost
as the entire roof caved in before them.

~

Appendix A: Illustrations

FIGURE 1. *The interior of the burned house.*

FIGURE 2. *A burial ground for dead stars.*

~

NOTES ON THE TEXT

This book owes a title debt to a sequence in Emily Toder's wonderful poetry collection, *Science*.

There are two different versions of the poem "Migration." The other version exists as part of a collaboration with Carol Guess entitled "Instructions for Staging."

I'm grateful to these writers for their inspiration.

ABOUT THE AUTHOR

Kristina Marie Darling is the author of ten previous books, which include *Melancholia (An Essay)* (Ravenna Press, 2012), *Petrarchan* (BlazeVOX Books, 2013), and (with Carol Guess) *X Marks the Dress: A Registry* (Gold Wake Press, forthcoming in 2014). Her work has been recognized with nominations for the PEN/Diamonstein-Spielvogel Award for the Art of the Essay, the San Francisco State University Poetry Center Book Award, and the Poetry Society of America's William Carlos Williams Book Award. Kristina's books have also been reviewed widely in literary journals, which include *The Colorado Review, Writers' Digest, Bookslut, The American Literary Review, Pleiades: A Journal of New Writing, Rattle: Poetry for the 21st Century, Stride Magazine* (U.K.), and *The Hiram Poetry Review*. Within the past few years, her writing has been honored with fellowships from the Corporation of Yaddo, the Hawthornden Castle International Retreat for Writers, the Helene Wurlitzer Foundation, the Virginia Center for the Creative Arts, the Vermont Studio Center, and the Ragdale Foundation, as well as grants from the Kittredge Fund and the Elizabeth George Foundation. Kristina is currently working toward a Ph.D. in Poetics at SUNY-Buffalo, where she holds a Presidential Fellowship.

21392918R00035

Made in the USA
Middletown, DE
27 June 2015